NARRATIVE OF THE LIFE OF FREDERICK DOUGLASS

A GRAPHIC CLASSIC BY
TERRY M. WEST

BASED ON THE AUTOBIOGRAPHY BY
FREDERICK DOUGLASS

SCHOLASTIC INC.

New York Toronto London Auckland Sydney
Mexico City New Delhi Hong Kong

PENCILLER
JAMAL IGLE

INKER
DAVID MOWRY

COLORIST
KURT MARQUART

LETTERER
JON OOSTING

COVER ARTIST
MICHAEL LILLY

COVER COLORS
J. BROWN AND TECH FX

Copyright © 1999 by Scholastic Inc.
All rights reserved. Published by Scholastic Inc.
Printed in the U.S.A.

ISBN 0-439-05702-7

SCHOLASTIC, READ 180, and associated logos and designs are trademarks and/or registered trademarks of Scholastic Inc.
LEXILE is a trademark of MetaMetrics, Inc.

10   06   05

NARRATIVE OF THE LIFE OF FREDERICK DOUGLASS

MANY CLASSIC BOOKS CAME FROM A WRITER'S IMAGINATION. THIS ONE CAME FROM REAL LIFE.

FREDERICK DOUGLASS GREW UP IN SLAVERY. FOR 20 YEARS, HE WORKED OTHER PEOPLE'S FARMS. HE CHOPPED OTHER PEOPLE'S WOOD. HE RAISED OTHER PEOPLE'S KIDS.

BUT IN 1838, HE ESCAPED. HE THEN WROTE A BOOK TO TELL ABOUT THE HORRORS OF BEING A SLAVE. HE WANTED TO CONVINCE PEOPLE THAT SLAVERY WAS WRONG.

THIS BOOK BECAME ONE OF THE MOST FAMOUS AUTOBIOGRAPHIES IN AMERICAN HISTORY.

"YOU HAVE SEEN HOW A MAN WAS MADE A SLAVE," FREDERICK DOUGLASS WROTE. "YOU SHALL SEE HOW A SLAVE WAS MADE A MAN."

I WAS BORN IN MARYLAND. I BARELY KNEW MY MOTHER. HER OWNER TOOK ME FROM HER WHEN I WAS A BABY. I'M NOT EVEN SURE HOW OLD I AM.

SLAVES KNOW AS MUCH ABOUT THEIR AGE AS HORSES DO.

MY MOTHER'S NAME WAS HARRIET BAILEY. I SAW HER ONLY FOUR OR FIVE TIMES WHEN I WAS A CHILD. SHE LIVED ABOUT 12 MILES AWAY.

SHE WORKED ALL DAY. THEN SHE WALKED TO SEE ME AT NIGHT. SHE SANG ME TO SLEEP. WHEN I WOKE UP, SHE WAS GONE.

I WAS TOO YOUNG TO WORK IN THE FIELDS. MY JOB WAS TO KEEP THE CHICKENS OUT OF THE GARDEN.

Be good! Or you'll feel my whip!

I WASN'T WHIPPED VERY OFTEN. BUT I WAS HUNGRY AND COLD A LOT.

AT NIGHT I HAD NO BED. I STOLE A LARGE CANVAS BAG. I WOULD CRAWL INTO IT ON THE COLD, DAMP FLOOR. THERE I WOULD SLEEP.

AT DINNER, THEY FED US BOILED CORNMEAL. IT WAS PLACED IN A LARGE WOODEN TRAY AND SET ON THE GROUND. THEN THEY CALLED THE CHILDREN TO EAT. THERE WAS NEVER ENOUGH.

WHEN I WAS SEVEN OR EIGHT, MY MASTER SENT ME AWAY.

You'll leave in a few days, Frederick.

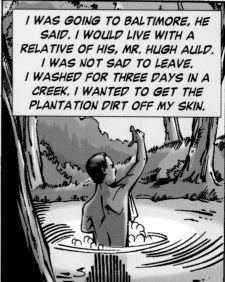

I WAS GOING TO BALTIMORE, HE SAID. I WOULD LIVE WITH A RELATIVE OF HIS, MR. HUGH AULD. I WAS NOT SAD TO LEAVE. I WASHED FOR THREE DAYS IN A CREEK. I WANTED TO GET THE PLANTATION DIRT OFF MY SKIN.

I GOT ON A BOAT HEADED FOR BALTIMORE.

AND I DID NOT LOOK BACK.

MR. AND MRS. AULD MET ME AT THE DOOR. THEIR LITTLE SON, THOMAS, WAS WITH THEM. MY JOB WAS TO LOOK AFTER HIM.

Welcome to our home, Frederick.

SOPHIA AULD DECIDED TO TEACH ME TO READ.

Soon *you* two will be reading to *me*!

SHE HAD NEVER HAD A SLAVE BEFORE. I WAS SHOCKED BY HER KINDNESS.

ONE DAY, MR. AULD FOUND OUT WHAT WAS GOING ON. HE TOLD HIS WIFE TO STOP TEACHING ME.

You cannot teach a slave to read! It's dangerous and against the law!

If you teach Frederick how to read, he will feel like he's equal to us.

He will be unhappy. He will think he shouldn't be a slave.

And he'll spread those ideas to the other slaves.

AULD'S WORDS SANK INTO MY HEART. NOW I UNDERSTOOD THE WAY TO FREEDOM. I HAD TO LEARN TO READ.

I WAS ABOUT 14 WHEN I WAS SENT BACK TO THE PLANTATION.

MY NEW MASTER WAS VERY CRUEL. HE KEPT US SLAVES HUNGRY.

You've gone soft from the city life! Now go get my horse!

HE WAS NEVER HAPPY WITH ME. I WAS ALWAYS LETTING HIS HORSE RUN OFF.

THIS WAS NOT AN ACCIDENT. IT WOULD RUN FIVE MILES TO ANOTHER FARM. I WOULD GO AFTER IT. WHEN I GOT THERE, I ALWAYS GOT SOMETHING GOOD TO EAT.

Don't worry. I'll teach this boy to obey!

MY MASTER COULDN'T STAND IT. HE SENT ME TO LIVE WITH A MAN NAMED EDWARD COVEY. COVEY WAS KNOWN FOR BREAKING THE SPIRITS OF SLAVES.

ONE DAY, MR. COVEY DECIDED TO TEACH ME A LESSON. HE CAME INTO THE STABLE WITH A LONG ROPE. HE PUSHED ME DOWN AND TRIED TO TIE ME UP. HE THOUGHT HE HAD ME.

What ... what are you doing?!

BUT I STILL HAD SOME SPIRIT.

I GRABBED HIM.

For six months you have beat me like an animal!

I don't care what happens. I won't take it anymore!

WE WERE AT IT FOR NEARLY TWO HOURS.

COVEY FINALLY LEFT ME ALONE.

13

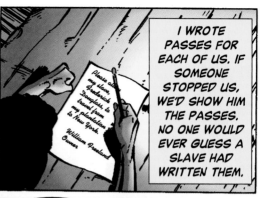

IN THE NORTH, SLAVERY WAS ILLEGAL. WE HAD TO GET THERE.

I WROTE PASSES FOR EACH OF US. IF SOMEONE STOPPED US, WE'D SHOW HIM THE PASSES. NO ONE WOULD EVER GUESS A SLAVE HAD WRITTEN THEM.

I'm afraid.

THE DAY OF OUR ESCAPE FINALLY CAME. WHEN I WOKE UP, I HAD A BAD FEELING. SOMETHING SEEMED WRONG.

I WAS RIGHT. SOMEONE HAD TOLD ON US. WE WERE ALL ARRESTED. WE WERE LUCKY THEY DID NOT HANG US.

I WAS RETURNED TO MY OLD MASTER. HE SENT ME BACK TO HUGH AND SOPHIA AULD IN BALTIMORE.

AULD GOT ME A JOB. AND HE KEPT MOST OF THE PAY.

Here's 12 dollars. It's what I earned this week.

Keep six cents for yourself.

STILL, I ALWAYS WORKED HARD. I WANTED MY MASTER TO THINK THAT I WAS HAPPY. I DIDN'T WANT HIM TO GUESS THAT I WAS PLANNING MY ESCAPE. THEN, ONE DAY, I WAS GONE....

BEFORE LONG, I MARRIED A WOMAN NAMED ANNA MURRAY. WE MOVED TO MASSACHUSETTS. THERE I TOOK ANY WORK I COULD FIND. I SAWED AND CARRIED WOOD. I SHOVELED COAL. I SWEPT CHIMNEYS.

I STARTED READING *THE LIBERATOR*. IT WAS AN ANTI-SLAVERY NEWSPAPER.

THE PAPER FILLED ME WITH JOY. IT SET MY SOUL ON FIRE. SOON, I WANTED TO DO MY PART TO END SLAVERY.

I WAS NERVOUS AT FIRST. BUT I KNEW I HAD TO TELL MY STORY. SO I BEGAN TO SPEAK AT ANTI-SLAVERY MEETINGS.

DATE DUE
